THE EROS OF REPENTANCE

Four Homilies
on the Theological Basis of Athonite Monasticism

THE EROS OF REPENTANCE

Four Homilies
on the Theological Basis of Athonite Monasticism

Archimandrite GEORGE KAPSANIS
of blessed memory,
ABBOT of the MONASTERY of
OSIOU GREGORIOU, MOUNT ATHOS

MONASTERY of OSIOU GREGORIOU
MOUNT ATHOS
2016

Pleroma Publishing
Glastonbury
BA6 9JQ
UK

Second and revised edition
© 2016 by the Monastery of Osiou Gregoriou, Mount Athos

All rights reserved. No part of this book may be reproduced, stored electronically or in any retrieval system, or transmitted in any form or by any means without prior written permission from the publisher.

British Library Cataloguing-in-Publication-Data
A record is available from the British Library

ISBN 978-0-9955103-2-6

To Blessed Father George
and the monks of Osiou Gregoriou,
who have so often opened their lives
to a troubled man of the world.

Mortals,
escape with me
from a false world!
Christ calls. Away!
Life be our voyage fair,
Safe riding o'er the surge of lies and care!
One quest alone employs the lonely monk;
How he may reach the haven of true peace
Where never comes the strain of breaking hearts.

O happy life, all music, free from sorrow!
Where is the prudent seeker of true gain
Who will part with all the world
and choose the cross?

Saint Theodore of Studion

CONTENTS

    PROLOGUE   1
    INTRODUCTION   2

I   The GOD-MAN as the IMAGE of GOD Teaches Man   5
       The Dynamism of the Image, Freedom and Eros
       Loss of the Image and its Recovery in Christ
       The Fellowship of Deification
       Modern Secularism, a False Alternative
       Traditional Orthodoxy, Our Answer & Our Responsibility

II   The THEOLOGICAL WITNESS of Mount ATHOS   15
       The Witness of True Repentance
       The Witness to a Living God
       The Witness to Theo-anthropocentric Life and Morals
       The Witness to an Orthodox Society
       The Witness to the Orthodox Faith
       Summary: Athos, the Cry of the Bride

III   EVANGELICAL MONASTICISM   33
       A New Life in Jesus Christ
       A Life of Repentance
       A Life of Prayer and Worship
       A Life Based on Love
       A Life of Service
       A Life of Charismatic Witness

IV   THEOTOKOS: GUIDE to TRUE FREEDOM   47
       (Christmas Address, 1986)

     GLOSSARY   51
     Words marked * in the text can be found in the Glossary.

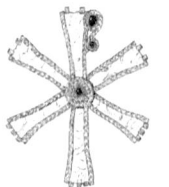

PROLOGUE
to the Second Edition

With the Grace of God we proceed to the second edition of this book, The Eros of Repentance. It was originally published in the 90s, but that English translation was unjust to the original. Now with the help of Andrew Walker of Pleroma Publishing, we offer to the English speaking world a new translation faithful to the original of our Elder of blessed memory Archimandrite George Kapsanis, as was first published in Greece.

The book comprises of four homilies. The first homily relates to the fact that, the God-man Christ teaches us as the Icon of God. The second homily explains that the theological witness of Mount Athos is a witness of real repentance, witness of the Living God, witness of a theo-anthropocentric life and of Orthodox faith. The third homily shows that Orthodox monasticism is the practical application of the evangelical teachings and life, which lead towards theosis through Grace. The fourth homily bears witness to the fact that the Virgin Mary, through her free assent and her co-operation in the Incarnation of the Logos, became our guide to the freedom of love.

The ascetical life in the Orthodox Church, in the monasteries and in the world, expresses our thirst for God. Repentance, the observance of the laws of Christ, cleansing of the passions, worthy communion in the divine Mysteries and in general the asceticism of the Church express this divine worship. The 'eros of repentance' is a God-given eros, a thirst of the divinely created man for his divine Archetype, the God-man Christ.

We beseech our Lord Jesus Christ to make us worthy to live theo-anthropocentrically in our holy Orthodox Church and to walk until the end the path of repentance, which leads to theosis, in which we are divinely called.

Archimandrite Christopher
Abbot of the Monastery of Osiou Gregoriou on Mount Athos
14th September 2016
The Feast of the Exaltation of the Precious and Life-giving Cross.

INTRODUCTION
to the Second Edition

The very title of this book will sound strange to modern man. On further reading, other words and concepts will also be new to most readers, but these are not new words or concepts, as they are expressions of original Christianity. A Christianity that has been here for two thousand years!

The original Christian and Biblical word for the immaterial part of man is psyche. In the talks that follow psyche is used. Initially readers may find this word strange; this should help the western reader to understand that Christianity in its pure and original form is very different to that which people understand today.

One problem with western Christianity is that this word has fragmented into two domains. We now almost exclusively talk of the healing of the psyche and of the salvation of the soul, and almost never the reverse. The soul remains in the domain of theology, whilst the psyche is now largely in the domain of medicine. Many westerners even perceive the psyche as a biological function, whereas, both soul and psyche pertain to the immaterial and immortal part of man.

4

I

The GOD-MAN as the IMAGE of GOD TEACHES MAN

The Orthodox theology of Christ as the image of God (2 Corinthians 4:4) and of man* as made 'according to the image of God' (Genesis 1:26) is fundamental to the proper understanding of what it means to be a human being.

The 'iconic character' of man, that is to say, to be made according to the image of God, signifies not only the special charismata (gifts) received from God, but also the goal of our existence – union with our Divine Archetype. 'Being as an Image' is the ontological principle of man – the Alpha and the Omega.

The Dynamism of the Image, Freedom and Eros

It has been correctly observed that man is a theological* being. As Panayiotis Nellas says: 'And to be a true man he must at every moment exist and live theocentrically. When he denies God he denies himself and destroys himself. When he lives theocentrically, he realises himself by reaching out into infinity; he attains his true fulfillment by extending into eternity.' (Panayiotis Nellas, *Deification in Christ*, St Vladimir's Seminary Press, 1987, p. 42)

Human existence owes its dynamism and its greatness to its 'iconic' character. In so far as we 'image forth' the wise

---
* See glossary

and creative God, we also possess the charismata (gifts) of knowledge and creativity.

In so far as we 'image forth' God who is free, we also possess free will and freedom. According to Saint Maximus the Confessor (d. AD 662): 'If we are made according to the image of the blessed and supersubstantial Divinity, and if the Divinity is by nature free, than we too, as a true image of the Divinity, are by nature free. If then we are by nature free, we possess the faculty of will.' (Migne, *Patrologia Greaca* 91, 304) If, according to Saint Nicholas Cabasilas, our free will is lost then our humanity is lost: 'It is the same to say that 'the free will is lost' as to say 'the human is lost.' (Migne, *Patrologia Greaca* 150, 638)

But what – more than anything else – reveals the divine imprint on the human being is the power of eros within the psyche* and this movement of eros towards its Divine Archetype.

According to Saint Maximus the Confessor, and Dionysius the Areopagite: 'At times scripture refers to God as eros (desire), and at other times as love, and at still other times as the desirable and beloved. Therefore, being Himself eros and love, He moves; while as desirable and beloved, He moves everything receptive to this eros and love towards Himself ... It is thus that the great apostle, Saint Paul, having come into possession of divine eros and become a participant of the ecstatic power, divinely inspired cries out: 'I live yet not I, but Christ lives in me.' He speaks as a true lover and –as he himself says– as one having tasted God's ecstatic power; no longer living his own life, but the Life of his Beloved, as exceedingly beloved.' (Translated from the original text of *The Philokalia of St Nicodemos*; cf. Saint Maximus the Confessor, *Various Texts on Theology,*

---
* See glossary

Century 5, par. 84-85; also in *The Philokalia*, G.E.H. Palmer, Philip Sherrard, Kallistos Ware, Vol. 2, 1990, pp. 280-281.) This power of eros within the psyche makes man thirst, from the depths of his existence, for unity with his Archetype: for theosis.* He does not find rest within created things and the finite. As Saint Nicholas Cabasilas says: 'The thirst of human souls needs, as it were, an infinite water; how then could this limited world suffice?' (*The Life in Christ*, see Migne, *Patrologia Greaca* 150, 638B)

We were created to be united with the uncreated Grace of God, to become ourselves gods by Grace. Here in a single view is the mystery of the human being as one 'commanded to be god'. (Saint Gregory the Theologian, *Funeral Oration on St. Basil the Great*, 47) According to Saint Gregory the Theologian: 'As the creator Logos* willed to fashion this – His own wealth of goodness – He creates man as a simple living being, from both invisible and visible nature ... and places him on earth as a kind of universe in miniature, another angel, a pilgrim blended of the two worlds, the overseer of the visible creation and the initiate of the spiritual, a king, ruling from above all things on earth ... a being, making its home here, yet translated elsewhere, and – the goal of the whole mystery – by his yearning for God, he is made god.' (Saint Gregory the Theologian, *Oration 45, On Holy Easter*, chapter 7)

Loss of the Image and its Recovery in Christ

With the fall of man, the image of God in him is darkened. Human nature, according to Saint Cyril of Alexandria, has been infected by sin.* As a result of this illness, that which is within us 'according to the image' is incapable of activating itself, of achieving the 'likeness of God'.

---

* See glossary

Jesus Christ, as the radiant and unchanged icon of God, and as the archetype of man, re-establishes the fallen image of Adam with His saving economy. He reveals our original beauty. He is also the good teacher Who re-orients, draws, and guides us toward our divine archetype.

The Church summarises this fact: 'Transfigured, Thou hast made the nature darkened in Adam radiant once again, O Christ, transforming it into the glory and brilliance of the Godhead.' (Vespers of the Transfiguration, celebrated August 6th)

When we thus become 'conformed to the image of Christ' (Romans 8:29) we acquire our real form, our genuine humanity.

The Fellowship of Theosis

In the holy Mysteries* and the Divine Liturgy, the union of God and man through our Lord Jesus Christ becomes communion with Life, resurrection, transfiguration, Christ-like transformation and theosis of the human.

That which is 'according to the image' is energised and the faithful and struggling human is deified. Theosis is not an idealistic desire, but reality.

First to be deified was the most holy Mother of God. According to our theologians she alone is found at the boundary between created and uncreated nature. She alone is god directly after God, and has the second place after the Holy Trinity. (St. Nicodemos the Athonite, *Unseen Warfare*, St. Vladimir's Seminary Press, Chapter 49) The saints possessing divine eros have also been deified. All the saints live the saying of Saint Ignatius the God bearer: 'My eros has been crucified.' (*Epistle of Saint Ignatius to the Romans*, Chapter 7)

---

* See glossary

The relation of the saints with God is the fruit of their divine eros, it is not merely ethical. The grace of theosis shines in their faces, and is revealed in their deified bodies which smell sweetly, give forth myrrh, remain uncorrupted, and work miracles. The Orthodox Church is the place and fellowship of theosis.

Whatever takes place in Orthodoxy is deifying, i.e. given to bring us into communion with God. The holy icons of Christ, of the Mother of God, of the saints, and all the decoration of our Orthodox Churches declare that, truly, 'God has become man in order to raise Adam up a god'. Theosis is possible because Grace is an uncreated and divine energy, able thus to deify us. Theosis is effected by God and 'suffered' by man. Deified man is purified from the passions. Attending to the prayer of the heart,* he receives an experience of divine Grace which refreshes and comforts him. A most exalted experience of theosis is the vision of the uncreated light of Mount Tabor. Deified people not only see this light supernaturally, but indeed they are themselves beheld within it – as has been witnessed in the life of Saint Basil. (St. Gregory of Nyssa, *Funeral Oration on Saint Basil the Great,* in Migne, *Patrologia Greaca,* 46, 809C)

Modern Secularism: A False Alternative

I believe that the above has great bearing on our conception of man and his education.

When human dynamism is not oriented in its proper direction, toward our Maker and Father, then it reveals itself negatively. The psyche is torn apart. The nous* is darkened. Man fed by the passions, hardens, becomes bestial and demonic.

---

* See glossary

According to Saint Gregory Palamas: 'A nous removed from God becomes like either a dumb beast or a demon. Once having transgressed the bounds of nature, it lusts for what is alien. Yet it finds no satisfaction for its greed and, giving itself the more fiercely to fleshly desires, it knows no bounds in its search for earthly pleasures.' (St. Gregory Palamas, *Oration 51*, chapter 6) The human being tumbles into 'non-being', which finally devours him. Dissolving, he falls to pieces. Life becomes a hell, freedom a burden, and other people a curse. The fate of man becomes tragic, with no hope of escape.

The mistake of secular humanism in all its shades is that it tries to make us forget our divine origin and purpose, our 'iconic' character. In the name of progress, of civilization, of justice, it imprisons us in what is corruptible, temporary, vain and passing. It cuts off our wings. It strives to confine our divinely-instilled dynamism and eros to worldly activities – which are not so much evil in themselves as insufficient: too limited to fulfil the desires of living beings who are made by God and destined for theosis. It also tries to persuade us that man is himself God, his own law, self-sufficient and self-fulfilling.

Here we arrive at the very sin of Adam: self-deification, egoism. Here we find the essence of secularist philosophy, ethics, and politics. This same philosophy attempts to organize daily life outside the Church. Secularism is the product of Western atheism, an illness that is now beginning to devour our own Orthodox people. The sad thing is that today there exist political philosophies which do not merely fight or tolerate the secularism that destroys our Orthodox tradition and identity, but in fact also have a programme to impose this secularism upon the people, using the mass media as their vehicle of choice.

Traditional Orthodoxy, our Answer and Responsibility

We must admit, however, that sometimes there is also an error from our side. Under the influence of Western Christianity, the Orthodox education of theosis is often replaced by the 'education of ethical improvement'.

The latter, a vision of natural and ethical deification, is man-centred. Even when it has a religious flavour, it still does not differ in essence from the ethical education of atheistic humanism. It is neither churchly nor liturgical. It does not reveal to the world human beings who are deified. Instead it produces (in Greece at least), 'small-town Christians': people limited to the bounds of propriety as they understand it. It is based on human ethical activity, and not on the action of God's uncreated Grace. It does not lead men out of their egocentricity, nor provide them with the experience of divine Grace. It does not impart divine eros, nor help them advance in true prayer and fellowship with God.

This approach made its first appearance in the Orthodox world some six hundred years ago. It was represented by the Western theologian Barlaam the Calabrian. By opposing him, Saint Gregory Palamas made himself the defender of the theology of uncreated Grace. Barlaam was defeated. However, his spirit has since returned in the form of the strong intellectual currents out of the West that have been 'flooding' into our Eastern European countries over the past two centuries.

Today we must become aware of the significant difference and opposition that exists between these two anthropologies and types of education: that which is represented by Barlaam, and that which we find in Saint Gregory Palamas and the *Philokalia*.

When our young people wake up from the lethargy of eudaemonism and humanistic self-deception, they begin to wander in search of a place to rest. A Christianity that is merely ethical cannot offer them peace. Their psyches thirst for a personal encounter and an experience of God, for a life that embodies a genuine mysticism, a redeemed and sanctified eros. If they cannot find true Orthodoxy, and cannot come to know our mystical theology, our real tradition and our genuine piety, then they will seek their resting places elsewhere – in the mysticisms of the Far East, for example, or in the much advertised self-transcendence provided by the artificial paradise of drugs ... or in the fogs and bogs of the occult.

The fact that the young people are not satisfied should disturb us, it should bring into question the quality of our teaching and training.

II

THE THEOLOGICAL WITNESS OF MOUNT ATHOS

The holy mountain of Athos in its entirety, both in its past and in its present, bears witness to Christ. Its witness is one of faith, hope, and love, a witness to life everlasting. This witness of true and evangelical life is thus also a theological witness: 'The accomplishment of purity is the foundation of theology', says Saint John Climacus. Permit me to draw attention to some aspects of this witness.

The Witness of True Repentance

Our Lord, the Incarnate Logos* made flesh, began His preaching with an invitation to repentance: 'And after John had been imprisoned, Jesus came to Galilee preaching the word of God and saying: 'The time is fulfilled and the Kingdom of God* is at hand. Repent and believe the Gospel.' (Mark 1:14–15) On Mount Athos, repentance* is experienced as the foundation of the Christian life. Someone once asked an elder of the Mountain: "What is the Holy Mountain?" He replied, "There is joy in heaven over one sinner who repents." Here we have many who repent.

Athos is indeed a place of repentance. Its monks have come here in order to live true repentance, to receive in themselves the depths of their own sinfulness, to suffer on account of it, to find assurance of the Lord's forgiveness, to

---

* See glossary

be cleansed of their passions.

Repentance is the daily struggle of the monk. His asceticism looks toward this one purpose: that he repent the more deeply and so is more pleasing to God. Repentance is the monk's 'science'. He does not repent just because he sinned against God at some time in the past. Rather, he feels intensely and every day that he cannot reply perfectly to God's love. He wants to offer himself completely to God, to be in perfect harmony with His commandments, and not to embitter Him with the slightest opposition to His will. Neither does the monk desire for even an instant to relax from the remembrance of God. As Saint Gregory the Theologian writes: 'Rather he should remember God even more than his breath.' Repentance is thus a dynamic condition, a continuous progress towards the Lord. Properly speaking, it is the pursuit of the Living God.

Its character is neither ethical nor legalistic. Instead, it is the fruit of a sanctified eros that strains toward the beloved Lord, a sign of profound humility and desire for God.

The younger monks on Athos learn from the older fathers who, even when they have attained a high degree of virtue, still repent and still mourn, so that they fulfil the word of the Lord: 'Blessed are those who mourn, for they shall be comforted. Blessed are those who weep now, for they shall laugh.' (Luke 6:21)

The holy elders instruct the younger men not by calling them to imitate their virtues, but by showing them how much they feel themselves to be sinners and unworthy. The joyful mourning of repentance is a way of life for the Athonite monk. Rarely do you find monks on Mount Athos who believe that they are virtuous, no matter how virtuous they may be.

In our monastery we were found worthy to have a holy elder, Father Auxentios, who died about ninety years of age. He passed away on the Sunday of Orthodoxy (the first Sunday into Great Lent) after the all night vigil and after 'Joyful Light' was chanted. Fr. Auxentios had reached a high level of sanctity and union with God. He none the less believed himself to be a great sinner. We would ask him, "What are you doing Father Auxentios?" And he would answer, "I swim in a sea of vanity, I don't know where I am or what I am doing, I have lost my senses."

Having this spirit of repentance, humility and simplicity the Athonite fathers do not make a pretence of being good. They are not hypocrites. They reveal what they are. They confess in all simplicity whatever temptation they consider sinful. If, as human beings of flesh and blood, they become the cause of any grief to a brother, they do not rest until they have bowed before him and sought his forgiveness before the day's end.

Our whole climate on Mount Athos calls us to repentance, to spiritual struggle, and to violence within ourselves for the sake of God's Kingdom. How could we rest when we meet daily, when we keep company with brethren who are holy, are prototypes of repentance; when every day so many examples of Christian perfections are set before us during the services. These demand that we struggle not for half-measures but for the perfection which the Lord commands.

One sign of true repentance is blessed compunction, the broken and contrite heart, the constantly flowing tears of those monks who have progressed in repentance. Very often such fruit cannot be hidden. This kind of repentance draws down the grace of God, secures the penitent, and brings peace and spiritual joy to his psyche. The same peace and joy greatly impress those who visit the Holy Mountain, and are able to discern these qualities in the faces of those monks who are so holy, yet outwardly deprived of life's pleasures.

A characteristic of the monk who lives in repentance is his attribution of every good thing to God and his dependence on divine grace for everything. He has been stripped of every human self-sufficiency, every confidence in self, and every desire to please himself. Those monks who possess the spirit of repentance and humility will normally withdraw from giving advice. Even should they do so, it will be out of love and obedience, and not because they feel themselves to be worthy so to do.

Should you ever visit or live for a time on Mount Athos, you will find yourself in a place of repentance, where human incapacities, imperfections, and sins may not be lacking, but in the overall scheme of things these are exceptions that are discordant and a sickness, from which the monk struggles to heal himself and to fulfil the commandments of the Saviour. On your visit to Mount Athos you also will feel the need to repent, to confess, to struggle.

It has often been observed that many of those who come to the Holy Mountain with no intention of confessing, will confess while they are there, and that while on the Mountain others who confess when in the world, find themselves confessing sins of which they had either been unaware or had not had the courage to confess before. There is indeed much joy in heaven when every day on Athos many sinners repent, both monks and pilgrims who, making their peace with God, become His friends. In this fashion the Holy Mountain makes its silent proclamation of repentance, and reminds us all that true repentance does not exhaust itself in ethical and pharisaic self-justification. Neither can it be divided up into single moments. Instead, it comprises the foundation of the whole of Christian life.

In today's world, humanism, psychology, pedagogy, and psychiatry – all of them based on a non-Orthodox Christian anthropology – ignore and are silent about the reality of sin.

Yet sin after the fall is an anthropological reality. It does not disappear because we try to persuade ourselves that it does not exist. There exists only one way for man, the creature of God, to find freedom from the guilt and weight of sin: through forgiveness by his Maker and Creator. Then, truly, man is at peace, liberated from the interior contradictions that create in him anxieties, neuroses and psychopathy. Then, indeed, he lives in the freedom of God.

The Witness to a Living God

When the monk possesses the grace of repentance, he knows the true God, and not some idea of God.

The God of the Gospels is Immanuel, 'God with us'. He is with us and we are capable of experiencing Him. Ours is not the unapproachable God of the philosophers. He is not the 'absolute being' of Western scholasticism. Rather, He is God who, while abiding unapproachable in His essence,* yet comes forth out of Himself by His divine energies and out of infinite love, to meet and unite Himself with man. The distinction between God's hidden being (His essence) and His active presence (His energies) has always been maintained by the Orthodox Church, as seen in the works of St. Basil the Great and other fathers. It was the Athonite saint, Gregory Palamas, who first taught this systematically in the fourteenth Century in order to defend the reality of the saints' experience of God as light, which the monk Barlaam, a westerner, had brought into question.

The Church, by the great Synods in Constantinople, vindicated St. Gregory and formally accepted his teachings, recognising in them its own faith. We feel it no exaggeration to say that this saint's teaching is a great blessing for the world. Why? Because it insists that the believer, once

---

* See glossary

having become cleansed of the passions and having become a participant in the holy mysteries, is able to receive direct experience of God, of seeing the uncreated Light of the Holy Trinity – the same light that the Apostles beheld at the Lord's Transfiguration on Mount Tabor. The believer can join with God and become a god through Grace. (Matthew 17:1-8; Mark 9:2-8; Luke 9:28-36)

God enters the cosmos through his uncreated energies. He thus endows it with existence, preserves and directs it. He is present in His creation.

If, however, God were essence, or being alone, without His divine energies, if Grace were a created thing – as Western Scholastics tell us – then man would be incapable of knowing Him directly, of seeing Him, of becoming a god himself, because created grace cannot deify a creature (created man). Neither could God Himself be present within creation, nor could He be personally at work within it. If uncreated Divine Grace is absent from nature, the inexorable laws of nature must replace it. So too, in the absence of uncreated Grace from the life of the Church and of Christians, it must be replaced by an ethical and legal system with a Pope as its head.

A God who does not deify man – such a God can have no interest for us, whether He exists or not. I believe that this goes far to explain the wave of atheism in the West, as well as the building of science and philosophy on an atheistic foundation. It is surely a sorry thing that we Orthodox, influenced by Western Europe, are also ignorant of and indeed sometimes even condemn Saint Gregory Palamas and other Fathers of the Church. This results in our substituting ethical conduct and a rationalistically idealist theology for the ascetical and pastoral Orthodox teaching of theosis. The former approach leads directly to a conventional Christianity and finally to atheism.

Many of our young people, weary of both materialism and ideology, are seeking mystical experience either in the teachings of oriental religions or in the artificial paradise of drugs, which in time become a living hell. Why this drift? Because they think that Orthodoxy is exclusively a matter of ceremonial and public declarations. They are ignorant of the mystical and neptic* tradition of the Philokalia, and of the prayer of the heart that bestows divine experience on believers: 'Blessed are the pure in heart, for they shall see God.' (Matthew 5:8)

Yet this way of prayer is still taught on Athos today. It is the discovery of the heart as the centre of our being, the cleansing of the passions, the turning of the nous to the heart, and the union of nous and heart with Christ, in order that vision of God may follow.

According to St. Gregory the Theologian, hesychia* deifies, because it helps us to truly know ourselves and also to know our God.

The Witness to Theo-anthropocentric** Life and Morals

Repentance and knowledge of the Living God permit the Christian, and particularly the monk of Athos, to direct his freedom toward the actual centre and source of life and the cosmos, the Triune God. Not to live anthropo-centrically, but theo-anthropocentrically, the centre of life being the God-man, Christ.

When someone lives a theo-anthropocentric life, he lives 'eucharistically'. That is to say he receives other people and the things of life as God's gifts to his life. He

---

* See glossary

** Theanthropokentrikos (θεανθρωποκεντρικός), which literally translates as 'God-man centred' – as opposed to the Western anthropo-centric world view.

then returns to the Lord thanksgiving, offering himself to God, and to God's children. In the bread and wine of the Eucharist, which are the gifts of God, the Christian offers his whole self and all that he has back to God. The bread and wine summarize what we are, and what we live by: 'Thine own of thine own we offer to Thee, through all and for all.' (from the Divine Liturgy, at the Elevation of Gifts)

The Lord receives our gifts and offers us in return His own Body and Blood, i.e. His Life. Thus the life of God becomes our life. As communicants of the divine life, we are enabled to live authentically ... truly spiritually.

Christ our God, who is sacrificed and offered for us, gives His Grace to the Christian as he partakes of the Eucharist, and so he helps him to attain to the similarity of the 'divine character': which is partaking in Christ's sacrifice and love, offering himself to his brethren. Therefore, to say that: 'I live theo-anthropocentrically', means that I live eucharistically, liturgically, ecclesiastically, sacrificially.

The spirit of our present age is anthropocentric. It is thus neither eucharistic, nor liturgical, nor sacrificial. It is not characterized by love of God or of brother, but love of self. Our whole civilization is built upon self-love.

It is natural, as long as Christians are influenced by this prevailing anthropocentricity, that they will live in a divided manner as a result. At certain times they behave 'religiously', (primarily while they are attending Church services), but at other times (outside the Church building), they act as if they were indifferent to the Faith. Religiosity itself, the manner of Christian piety, departs from the traditional churchly and Orthodox way; it becomes instead individualistic and sentimental. The liturgical life and worship of the Church are seen as something good but as of secondary importance. We no longer come to perceive that – outside the Liturgy and the Church's worship – the world is incapable of being unified and transfigured in newness of life. We attempt to replace the activity of God in the Church and her liturgical life with our own activity on behalf of the world, whether solely through excessive social action or political struggle. We try to make the Church an instrument for helping and improving the world, when in fact it is for the world to become Church, to be grafted into the Body of Christ, to die and so to be raised up.

Behind this state of affairs lies our wish to be accepted by our secularised society. The latter does accept, even applauds people of the Church, when they work according to the world's agenda – instead of to the Church's agenda.

Western humanism has altered the perception of many Orthodox people. So much is this so that we are no longer sensitive to the spiritual tradition of our God-bearing Fathers, of monasticism, ecclesiastical art and chant, iconography, architecture, the conciliar function of the Church's body, the holy canons, the dogmas, and the true piety of Orthodoxy. Through this alteration, neither we nor the surrounding world are 'made Church', nor are we saved: 'what is not assumed is not healed'. We remain scattered, we do not live our unity in Christ; not in ourselves nor with the surrounding world.

On Mount Athos, by the grace of God, the theo-anthropocentric tradition of the Church as life and way of life is preserved. The heart of the Tradition is the Holy Trinity in Christ. The purpose of the Tradition is union with God. All of life is referred to and finds its centre in God. The Divine Liturgy is celebrated daily. Worship occupies the first place. Work, duties, eating, hospitality – all begin from, and return to, the Holy Eucharist. Everything becomes eucharistic, with thanksgiving. The location of the main Church in the physical centre of the compound, and the ordering of all the buildings around that central altar reveal this fact.

The monk remains in continuous union with our beloved Lord, through his unceasing practice of the Jesus prayer, 'Lord Jesus Christ, have mercy on me a sinner'. Thus he unites the faculties of his psyche, so that even at work he struggles to pray. All of this means that 'Christ might be all, and in all'. As Saint Symeon of Thessalonica writes: 'For he is a Christian who is wholly with Christ, thinking about Christ ... and in relation to Christ studying, caring, living, and being moved to act. He breathes only Christ, and carries Him about with himself, neither having nor desiring anything save Christ. As did the Apostle Paul, he holds Christ alone as his reward. Christ is to him the pearl of great price, his great treasure and life and light, his sweetness and kingdom everlasting.'

The piety of the Athonite monks towards our Lady the Theotokos,* the Custodian of Mount Athos, also has a Christocentric character. For whoever loves the Son cannot help but love the Mother. And our Mother helps us to love the Son.

Should one find oneself on the Holy Mountain of Athos, he would discover a new way of perceiving; a whole different world with different standards, different goals belonging to another kingdom – indeed, to the Kingdom* that is to come. We say that he shares in and tastes the Kingdom.

At this point he becomes aware that the anthropocentric standards and goals of the world cannot be salvific – cannot save. He senses the necessity of conforming his own life to the standards of Athos, standards that are none other than the theo-anthropocentric standards of Orthodoxy. It is in this fashion that the lives of many pilgrims to Athos have been changed. After their pilgrimages they begin to practice a Christianity that is more Churchly, more traditional – more Orthodox – than before.

---

* See glossary

The same people also uncover the meaning of many of the Church's rules and traditions, of which they had previously been ignorant or simply ignored: rules and traditions of liturgical life, of fasting, vigil, prayer of the heart, and of stillness as the precondition of prayer. Certainly, Christians in the world cannot live precisely as monks. They can however live in accordance with the spirit and standards of monastic life. This will aid them greatly in preserving their own inner unity and balance while living in a troubled and anxious world.

The Witness to an Orthodox Society

The Holy Mountain bears witness to the hidden life in Christ. At the same time, its testimony is to the evangelical manner of organizing life in society. This is no paradox. In a very essential way, interior life is also social life, since through it a man truly communicates with God and with his fellows. As we read in the Acts of the Apostles: 'And all that believed were together and had all things in common, and sold their possessions and goods and parted them to all men, as every man had need. And they, continuing daily with one accord in the temple, and breaking bread from house to house, did eat their food with gladness and singleness of heart, praising God and having favour with the people.' (Acts 2:44 - 47)

This blessed common society of the Jerusalem Christians still continues, by the Grace of God, in the common-life (cœnobitic) monasteries, which form the foundation of monasticism on Mount Athos. Here the tables of the refectory are set daily with love not only for the monks, but also for the flood of pilgrims and visitors who come to the holy places. This occurs only on Mount Athos, and it occurs because of the sacrifice and labour of the brothers. Here we divide our spiritual and material goods with our brethren in the name of Christ. You will find that on Athos the Church is not a closed circle where others have no place, but rather as it appears on the icon for the feast of Pentecost, an open hemisphere, a welcoming embrace, which invites and has room for all the world.

Saint Basil the Great, legislator and theologian of the common monastic life, writes concerning the Christian society: '... I call that a most perfect community of life in which private property has been expelled, conflict of will chased away, where every kind of turbulence, aggression, and quarrel has been trampled under foot; but where instead all is in common; souls, wills, bodies, and everything which is required for the nurture and care of bodies, where God is in common. Common are the goods of piety, salvation in common, common are the struggles, the labours, and the crowns, where the many are one and the one is not alone but among many. Where is the equal of this way of life? What is there greater? ... All are equally servants and lords of one another ... love itself subordinating them one to another ...'

Thus do the monks return again through love to the condition of Adam before the fall, when sin had not yet broken up the unified nature of man. They imitate precisely the life of Christ with the choir of the Apostles, 'where all is common', and where to the Apostles in common Christ provided himself. They are zealous for the life of the angels, 'preserving all in common just as the latter.'

The unity of the monks reveals to men how many good things the incarnation of the Saviour has brought to us: 'For this is the sum of the Saviour's economy according to the flesh, that He might join human nature to itself and to Himself, removing the cleft wrought by evil and recalling the original union, just as some wonderful physician might take a body cut in pieces, and with saving medicines bind it again together, and make it alive.' Saint Basil's theological and Christological perspective on the common life is preeminent. He always speaks of the common life as anchored in the rock that is Christ.

It is relative to this love, unity, and possession in common that Christian societies in the world must orient themselves if they wish to fulfil the Gospel of Christ. In the common life of monasticism, one may find the principles for the saving solution of our social problems, a true and human solution that will not overlook the spiritual and God-like nature of man. The monk who is voluntarily humble, without private possessions, and subordinate to obedience – all after the example of the Saviour – proclaims to the world silently yet with great force the realities of faith, sacrifice, humility, love, justice, and peace as the prerequisites for true freedom.

The Witness to the Orthodox Faith

The witness of the Holy Mountain is also precious as it concerns themes relating to Orthodox faith. The struggle of the Holy Fathers of our Church was to preserve the Faith as it was delivered to them, without innovation. They knew that any 'forgery' in this realm, be it ever so small, leads to greater forgeries, and that dogma, once it errs, leads to a mistaken life and pastorate. This is gambling with man's salvation.

Today, under the influence of secularisation, the dogma and traditional Orthodox ecclesiology are overlooked. The union of the 'churches' is being pursued along practical and pragmatic lines, without thought for the necessary unity in Faith. One Athonite elder has said, wisely and simply, 'the dogmas are not for the Common Market'. Another has said: 'How can we accept the Latins without their changing in any regard, while at the same time we light the lamp every day at the icon on the spot where the martyr-monks who reproved the Latinisers were put to death? These martyrs we honour as saints.' The Fathers of the Holy Mountain often say as well: 'If we should be silent about the Faith which is in danger, how can we explain to ourselves our sitting so many years on this rock?'

It is a fact that whoever struggles for precision in the life in Christ is also sensitive to the dogmas of the Orthodox faith. The monks have the experience of Truth,** who is Christ the Incarnate Logos. They cannot be dissuaded from this Truth in its dogmatic formulation. The Church has always taken account of this sensitivity of the monks. Wise and holy monks – men such as Saint Maximus the Confessor – have stood as pillars and exemplars of the Orthodox Faith, and directed the work of Œcumenical Councils.

It was not only St. Gregory Palamas, but many other Athonite monks were also called to take part in large Councils of the Ecumenical Patriarchate to bear witness to the Orthodox faith.

See what the great saint and luminary of the Church, Theodore the Studite, says: 'If, then, there are real monks in the present times, let them be proven by their works. The work of the monk is not to tolerate in the slightest innovations concerning the Gospel, because in setting an example of heresy for the laity and keeping company with heretics they will be obliged to give account for the destruction of the faithful.'

Elsewhere the same saint writes: '... And overlooking others, let me come to the present generation and the heresy that confronts us now. Who have resisted unto blood, struggling against sin, if not our blessed Fathers and brothers of this and of other monasteries? Such then are the accomplishments and victories of the monks, and monks

---

** In the original text Ὑποστατικὴ Ἀλήθεια (Hypostatic Truth) relates to the Person of Jesus Christ.

are the nerves and foundation of the Church. Such indeed and so great is the dignity with which we have been graced by the goodness of God.'

The struggle of the Athonites is not simply directed against heresy. It is a struggle to realise in themselves – and to make manifest – the fullness of the Truth and the Life possessed by the Church. The pain, the unease, the protests of the Holy Mountain are in essence elements of the struggle for fullness, for catholicity. It is in order that the preaching of the Cross not be emptied, that the Gospel not be counterfeited. In the words of Saint Gregory the Theologian, we must not theologise in the manner of Aristotle (i.e. scholastically), but according to the fishermen (i.e. apostolically). Athos bears its witness in order that we do not lose the possibility of theosis and of the Uncreated Light by accepting grace as a created thing; that the Church does not fall from being the 'Body of Christ' to become some human organisation; so that some 'infallible' Pope does not come to replace the truly infallible and ever-present, illuminating and uncreated Grace of the Holy Spirit. This Grace is always with the Church.

For these reasons, by the Grace of God, we, together with the holy bishops, clergy, and faithful people, shall never agree that there should come about the least alteration in the dogmas of piety. We take this attitude out of love: love for the God of Truth and for the non-Orthodox who are not helped when they are prevented from coming into confrontation with the Truth which saves: 'You will know the Truth, and the Truth shall make you free.' (John 8:32)

Summary: Athos, the Cry of the Bride

One cannot know the Holy Mountain with one or two visits. It is even less possible for someone to know it if he approaches it with the proud logic of the world: 'Blessed are the poor in spirit, for theirs is the Kingdom of heaven.' (Matthew 5:3)

As far as the Athonite monk is poor, the deeper he is initiated into the mystery of the Holy Mountain. When Jacob saw the ladder that led to God and the angels who ascended and descended from heaven, he said: 'How fearful is this place! Is this not the house of God and this the gate of heaven?'(Genesis 28:17) Jacob wrestled with God. On Athos the monks wrestle with God. They speak with God, with the Mother of God, with the saints. Thus they truly witness to God and to His love in Christ for the world.

Perhaps the most essential witness of Mount Athos cannot be expressed by words. However, all of us perceive that Mount Athos is more meaningful than some huge outdoor museum of Byzantine art and civilization. It is the dew of Hermon descending on the mountains of Zion. It is the comfort of our hearts, a lamp at our feet. We feel as well that Athos does not live for itself, but for the Church. It is God's gift to the Church – and the Church's gift to God. It is not above the Church, but a manifestation of the Church. Praise of the Holy Mountain is praise of our Mother, the Church.

Now that everything around us is being shaken to its foundations, the search for the authentic is a matter of life and death.

Our people will not be saved by westernisation, which fast progresses. This will only bring more stress, emptiness, disintegration and destabilisation. Drug abuse, suicide and neurosis will increase. It is our youth who will pay the greatest cost, because they are the most sensitive and susceptible.

A foreign ambassador stationed in Athens, some time ago on his visit to Mount Athos told me: "We in the west find ourselves at an impasse. In the place of God, we have placed man himself, now he also has fallen and we find ourselves facing chaos. I find my solution in the Eastern Fathers. I translate St. Maximos the Confessor into my own language. I am saddened to see Greek intellectuals focusing solely on the classical writers and not progressing to the Church Fathers." It seems that this verification by the foreign ambassador reveals our sickness from 1821 (the birth of the modern Greek state) onwards. Theology, politics, education and intellectualism by and large have ignored the Church Fathers. They are based on alien models. They have not expressed the psyche of our Greek Orthodox people. They remain spiritually strangers to our people.

Thank God, it now seems that a certain awakening is happening and a return to the Fathers. This also explains the return to monasticism.

Athos keeps vigil, serves, is silent, and prays. On the Holy Mountain one may hear the cry of the Bride to her Bridegroom: 'And the Spirit and the Bride say, Come. And let him that heareth say, Come. And let him that is athirst, come. And whosoever will, let him take the water of life freely ... He which testifieth these things saith, surely I come quickly. Amen. Even so, come, Lord Jesus.' (Revelation 20:17–20)

32

III

EVANGELICAL MONASTICISM

A New Life in Jesus Christ

The Gospel of our Lord Jesus Christ is 'good news' because it brings to the world something that is not merely new teaching, but a new life in contrast to the old. The old life is ruled by sin, passions, corruption and death, and is presided over by the devil. In spite of all its 'natural' pleasures it still leaves a bitter taste, because it is not true life, the life for which man was made, but a corrupted life, diseased, characterised by a sense of the irrational, of emptiness, and of anxiety.

The new life is offered to the world by the God-man Christ as a gift and a possibility for all men. The believer is united with Jesus Christ, and thus partakes of His divine and immortal life, that is, of everlasting or true life.

A Life of Repentance

In order for the believer to be joined to Christ and to be made alive, he must first die to the old man by means of repentance. One must crucify and bury the old man, (that is, egoism, the passions, and the selfish will) at the cross and tomb of Christ, in order to rise with Him and walk in 'newness of life' (Romans 6:4). This is the work of repentance and the carrying of the cross of Christ. Without repentance, which is the continual crucifying of the old man, the believer is incapable of believing evangelically. He cannot give himself entirely to God and 'love the Lord with all his heart, and all his psyche, and all his mind and all his strength'. (Mark 12:30)

It is for this reason that the Lord Himself set forth as the foundation of His preaching and, as the basis of faith, repentance: 'repent, and believe in the Gospel.' (Mark 1:15) He did not hide the fact that the life of repentance is a difficult and uphill struggle: 'Narrow is the gate and hard is the way which leads to life.' (Matthew 7:14)

To walk this way means to lift up the cross of repentance. The old man does not give way without violence, and the devil is not conquered without hard warfare.

The monk promises to follow throughout his life the narrow and hard way of repentance. He breaks away from the things of the world in order to achieve the one thing that he desires. He dies in relation to the old life, that he may live the new one that Christ offers him in the Church. The monk pursues perfect repentance by means of continual asceticism: vigils, fasting, prayer, the cutting away of his will, and unquestioning obedience to his elder. In the practice of these he forces himself to deny his private and selfish will, and to love God's will. A monk is 'a perpetual forcing of nature'. The word of the Lord is thus fulfilled: 'The kingdom of heaven is taken by violence, and the violent take it by force'. (Matthew 11:12)

In the midst of the birth-pangs of repentance, the new man according to God is slowly begotten. The struggle of repentance includes the effort of continuously guarding one's thoughts. This will eliminate all evil and demonic temptations that want to contaminate us. In doing so, we keep clean the heart, so as to see God. In the Beatitudes our Lord says: 'Blessed are the pure in heart, for they shall see God.' (Matthew 5:8)

Victory over egoism and the passions makes the monk calm, meek, and humble, in short – 'poor in spirit' – and a participant in all virtues of the Beatitudes. It also makes him a 'child', like that child which Jesus blessed and whom He called on all to imitate if they wished to enter His kingdom.

The whole life of the monk becomes a study of repentance, his way of life a way of repentance. A monk is a scientist of repentance, one who is 'branded with the life of repentance' (Canon 43, 6th Œcumenical Council) for the whole Church. Contrition and the tears of repentance are the most eloquent sermon.

In addition, the monk's whole manner of life, the way of self-mortification, is a judgement of the world. Silently judged, the world that does not take part in the monk's repentance rejects him, hates him, despises him, and sees him as a fool. Yet, with such men, 'foolish, weak, ignoble and rejected of the world', God confounds the wise. (I Corinthians 1:27)

A monk who is wise according to God and foolish according to the world remains a stranger in the world, as was the Son of God. 'He comes to his own and his own do not receive him.' (John 1:11) His own do not understand him, nor the wise and the diligent, nor sometimes even the people of the Church.

For those who do not partake of his spirit, the monk's hidden and secret life is a mystery sealed with seven seals. Those who do not share in this see him as no use either for society or for the missionary work of the Church. His life is hidden with Christ in God, though it shall be 'revealed in glory with the coming of Christ'. (Colossians 3:4)

Only if the heart of a man is continually being purified of egoism, of selfishness, and of the passions, is it capable of truly loving God and man. Egotism and love are incompatible. The egotist may often think that he loves, but in fact his 'love' is merely a disguised egotism, hiding his selfishness and self-interest.

The repentant monk is aflame with divine desire. Love of God possesses his heart. He can no longer live for himself, but only for God. Like a bride, the monk's psyche longs continuously with pain and yearning for the Bridegroom. It cannot rest until it is united with Him. The monk finds no peace in loving God as would a servant – from fear – nor as a hired hand, for the sake of the reward of paradise: he wants to love Him as a son, from a pure heart. 'I no longer fear God, because I love Him', says Saint Anthony the Great.

The more the monk repents, the more his desire grows for the love of God. The more he loves God, the more deeply he repents.

A Life of Prayer and Worship

Tears of repentance kindle the fire of love. The monk feeds his desire for the Lord with prayer, especially that noetic and unceasing prayer which is the continual invocation of the sweetest name of Jesus. The prayer, 'Lord Jesus Christ, Son of God, have mercy on me, a sinner' both purifies and establishes him in union with Christ.

Worshiping in Church, the monk also gives himself lovingly to God, and God gives himself back to him. The monk spends many hours every day worshiping his beloved Lord in the Temple. His participation in worship is not an 'obligation', but rather a necessity of his psyche which thirsts for God. In Athonite monasteries the Divine Liturgy is celebrated every day. The monks do not rush to finish the service, no matter how lengthy; for they know nothing better than to be in communion with the Redeemer, the Mother of the Redeemer, and the friends of the Redeemer. Worship is a joy and a festival, springtime of the psyche, a foretaste of

Paradise. The monks live, in other words, according to the way of the Apostles: 'And all that believed were together, and had all things common ... and they, continuing daily with one accord in the Temple and breaking bread from house to house, did eat their food with gladness and singleness of heart, praising God ...' (Acts 2:44-47)

And after the dismissal of the service, the monk lives worshipfully: his whole life in the monastery, the service which he performs, the refectory, prayer, silence and rest, his relations with the brethren, and the reception of guests, are offered as liturgy to the Holy Trinity.

The architecture itself of the monasteries bears witness to this reality. From the Church and its holy altar, all things proceed, and to them all things return. The corridors, the cells, everything is centred on the Catholicon (the central church or temple of the monastery) as a hub.

All of life is offered to God, and becomes worship. The material elements used in the worship witness to the Transfiguration of all life, and of the whole creation by God's grace. The bread and wine of the Divine Eucharist, the sanctified oil, the incense, the sounding-boards ('semantrons') and bells which announce the appointed hours, the candles and the oil lamps which are lit and extinguished at certain times of the service, the movement of the canonarch and the ecclesiarch, and as many other movements and activities as are provided by the age-old monastic 'typika' (rules), are not mere symbols, nor are they psychological props intended to generate sentimental feelings. Instead, they are signs, echoes, and actual manifestations of the New Creation. Everyone, as many as visit the Holy Mountain, discovers that its worship is not static, but possesses a dynamic character. It is a single motion toward God: together with itself, the psyche that ascends to God raises up all creation.

In the Athonite vigil, the believer has a unique

experience of joy, which comes into the world from the redemptive work of Christ.

The believer thus tastes of the highest quality of that life which Christ offers within the Church to the world. The priority which monasticism gives to the worship of God is a reminder, both in the Church and in the world, that if the Divine Liturgy and worship do not once again become the centre of our life, our world will be unable to be united and transfigured. It will be incapable of surpassing its divisions, its imbalance, its emptiness and death ... in spite of all the prideful, humanistic systems and plans intended to improve it.

Again, monasticism reminds us that the Divine Liturgy and worship are not simply one thing amongst others in our life: they are its centre, the source of its renewal and sanctification of all areas of our life.

A Life Based on Love

The love of God has – as a direct fruit – the love of God's image, of man, and of all God's creation. After many years of asceticism, the monk acquires the 'merciful heart' which loves as God does. According to Abba Isaac the Syrian, a merciful heart is '... a burning of the heart for all creation, whether for men, for the birds of the air, for animals, for the demons, for every creature. From the memory and contemplation of creatures the eyes stream with tears, and from compassion and pity the heart of the merciful man is moved to grief, and is unable to bear, to see, or to hear of any injury, or of anything grievous occurring in creation. It is for this reason that at all times such a man prays with tears for the dumb beasts, for the enemies of the truth, and for those who do him injury. He prays that God may protect them and show them mercy. He prays even for the creeping things, out of his great pity, which moves his heart abundantly.' (*Discourse 81*)

In the *Gerontikon*, (a collection of sayings and works of the Desert Fathers, or 'Elders'), we encounter forms of sacrifice and love which call to mind and manifest the love of Christ. It is mentioned that Abba Agathon said: 'I wish to meet a leper and embrace his body.' Saint Isaac the Syrian commented, 'Do you see perfect love?'

The organisation of the cœnobitic monastery is based on love, according to the model of the first Christian communities of Jerusalem. As the Lord with the twelve, and as the first Christians, so monks too have all things in common in Christ. The abbot possesses nothing more than the newest novice. No one has money that he may spend as he wishes, only those funds which he takes as a blessing from the abbot for a particular need.

The possession of all things in common, equality, justice, reciprocal reverence, and the sacrifice of one for all, and of all for each, raises the common life to the level of real love and liberty. As many as have lived, be it only for a few days, in true common-life monasteries, know what a joy is the reciprocal love of the brethren, and how much it refreshes the psyche. One has the impression that he is living with the angels.

The organiser of common-life monasticism, Basil the Great, speaking characteristically about the love in Christ which rules in the cœnobia, said: 'What can compare with this form of life? What is more blessed? What is truer than its binding together and its unity? What is more joyful than the blending of personalities and psyches? Men have been moved to come from different tribes and countries to be joined together so truly into one that they appear as one psyche having many bodies; like instruments of a single will. The one who is weak in body has many who bear with him; the one who is ill and frail in his psyche has many to care for him and set him aright. They are equally servants one of another, equally lords one over the other, and with unconquerable liberty they strive to show among themselves the greatest servitude. Theirs is a servitude, however, which is not forced out of some necessity of the kind that causes great anxiety for those who rule, but is rather created out of the joy that comes from freedom of the will. Love leads each man to subordinate himself to the other, and establishes freedom in the individual choice of each. It is thus that God willed us to be from the beginning; for this He created us. Such men restore the ancient beauty, because they redeem the sin of the forefather Adam... because there would not have been division, separation, and war among men if sin had not divided nature. These men, then, imitate the Saviour and His incarnate life.

Just as He did when He formed the band of His disciples, establishing all things in common among the Apostles, even giving of Himself, so the monks that keep the strictness of this life imitate the life of the Apostles and of the Lord by the obedience to the abbot. They are zealous for the life of the angels and in following their example, they strictly guard the common life. Among the angels there is neither strife, nor envy, nor dispute. All things belong to each, and all store up for one another those things which are good.' (*Constitutiones Asceticae*, 18, 2)

A Life of Service

In monasteries of the common-life, the monks are able to live apostolically, genuinely, the mystery of the Church as the mystery of communion and union of God and men. They are able to live 'the unity of the faith and the communion of the Holy Spirit', which is the petition of all Christians. The monk knows from experience that the Church is not a religious institution, nor a law, but brotherhood in Christ, the Body of Christ, the gathering together of the formerly scattered children of God (John 11:52), his family in Christ. This experience of the Church gives the monk his capacity to see his brothers as members of his own body, and to honour them as Christ. This explains the ready welcome which he extends to pilgrims and visitors, as well as his continual prayers with tears on behalf of his brethren, both living and dead, both known and unknown.

The monks also fulfil their love for their brethren in the world in other ways, such as by the spiritual refreshment and comfort that they offer to their brothers. Many who are troubled and tired in their psyche run to the monasteries, particularly to the Holy Mountain, to find peace for their psyche in proximity to elders and confessors who have already found peace with God. On the other hand, those occasions are not rare where experienced Athonite confessors go out into the world, refreshing and confirming many Christians in the faith.

The venerable Seraphim of Sarov, a great Russian saint of the last century, says typically: 'Be yourself at peace with God, and many will come to find peace near you.'

The venerable Seraphim was speaking from his personal experience, as well as from the experience of the long spiritual tradition of the Church. It is an observed fact that the further those elders who had found peace with God retreated into the desert, the more the multitudes followed them in order to be edified.

In special circumstances, monks are called by the Lord Himself to take up a broader work of preaching and awakening, as occurred with Saint Cosmas the Aetolian. But they are always called by God, and never call themselves. It would have been impossible for Saint Cosmas to save and to enlighten an enslaved people with his preaching if he had not previously been enlightened and illumined by the twenty years of monastic practice, silence, purification and prayer.

The monk does not seek to save the world through pastoral or missionary activity because, being 'poor in spirit', he feels that he does not have the prerequisites for saving others prior to his own salvation. He gives himself to God without plans or hopes for the future. He is always at the disposal of the Lord, ready to attend to His call.

The Lord of the Church invites the workers of his vineyard to work in whatever mode He finds salvific and edifying. He called Saint Gregory Palamas to take up the pastoral protection of the Thessalonians, and to give authentic expression of the theology of the Fathers.

He called Saint Cosmas to go out and preach in apostolic journeys, while he illumined Saint Nicodemus the Hagiorite to preach without going out into the world – by means of the theological and spiritual writings that to this very day lead many psyches to God. Other monks were called by the Lord to edify the world with their silence and endurance, by their prayers and their tears, as in the case of the blessed Leontius of Dionysiou. This Athonite did not go out of his monastery for sixty years. He remained all that time closed within a dark cell. The Lord revealed His acceptance of this offering, by giving him the gift of prophecy. After his death his body gave forth myrrh.

A Life of Charismatic Witness

Properly speaking, what makes the sanctified monk the world's joy and light is his preservation of the image of God.

In the midst of the unnatural condition of sin in which we live, we forget and lose sight of the measure of the true man. That which man was before the fall, and that which is man deified – that is, the image of God – this is what the sanctified monk reveals to us.

For those who are able to discern the deeper and true human nature, without the prejudices of passing ideologies, the monk remains the hope of mankind. If man cannot be deified – and if we have not personally known deified men – it would be difficult to hope in the possibility that man can surpass his fallen condition, can attain to the purpose for which the good God made him: theosis, by grace. As John of the Ladder says: 'The angels are light for monks, and monastic life is light to all men.'(Saint John Climacus, *Discourse 26*)

Already possessing the grace of theosis in this life, the monk becomes a sign and witness of the Kingdom of God in the world. According to the holy Fathers, the Kingdom of God is the gift and indwelling of the Holy Spirit. By means of the deified monk, the world is given to know 'in ignorance' – to see 'without seeing' – the character and glory of the deified man and of the Kingdom of God which is to come, and which is not of this world.

It is through monasticism that the eschatological conscience of the Apostolic Church is preserved in the Church of today. By eschatological conscience, we mean both eagerly awaiting the coming of the Lord (*marana tha*: Lord, come!), and the awareness of His mystical presence among us: 'The Kingdom of God is within us.'

His charismatic remembrance of death and his fruitful virginity extend the monk into the age to come. As Saint Gregory the Theologian teaches: 'Christ is born of the Virgin Mary, and establishes virginity as that which leads us out of the world, cuts off the world, exchanges one world for another, the present world for the world to come ... turning from that which is seen, to that which is unseen.' The monk who lives the life of virginity according to Christ transcends not only that which is unnatural, but nature itself. Attaining to that which is beyond nature, he partakes of the angelic mode of being which transcends gender, of which the Lord also spoke: 'For in the resurrection they are neither married nor given in marriage, but are as the angels of God in heaven.' (Matthew 22:30) Just as are the angels, so the monks are also not virgins in order to accomplish matters of practical importance for the Church (missionary work, etc.), but in order to worship God 'in their body and spirit'. (I Corinthians 6:20)

Virginity sets a boundary to death. In the words of Saint Gregory of Nyssa: 'Just as in the case of the Theotokos, Mary, death which had reigned from Adam until her stumbled against the fruit of her virginity as at a rock when it came against her, and shattered round about her; so in the case of every psyche which passes through this fleshly life in virginity, the power of death is somehow shattered and abolished, as having nowhere to insert its sting.' (*On Virginity*, chapter 14)

The evangelical and eschatological spirit which is preserved by monasticism serves to protect the Church in the world from secularisation and from allying itself with sinful conditions which are antithetical to the evangelical spirit.

Physically isolated and silent, but spiritually and mystically in the midst of the Church, the monk preaches as from an elevated pulpit the precepts of Almighty God and the necessity for a wholly Christian life. He orients the world toward the Jerusalem that is on high, and toward the glory of the Holy Trinity as the true and universal goal of creation. This is the apostolic preaching which monasticism has authentically preached in every epoch, which grounds the apostolic renunciation of all things in the crucified life of apostolic work. Just as the Holy Apostles, even so the monks, 'having abandoned all things', follow Jesus and fulfil His word: 'Everyone who leaves houses, or brothers, or sisters, or father, or mother, or wife, or children, or fields for my Name's sake, shall receive an hundredfold and shall inherit life everlasting.' (Matthew 19:29)

'Owning nothing and possessing all things' (II Corinthians 2:10), the monks share in the sufferings, the deprivations, the hardships, the vigils, and the worldly insecurity of the Holy Apostles. They are made worthy, however, as were the Holy Apostles, of becoming 'eyewitnesses of His Majesty' (II Peter 1:16), and of receiving personal experience of the grace of the Holy Spirit, so that they are enabled to say not only that: 'Jesus Christ came into the world to save sinners, of whom I am first' (I Timothy 1:15), but also: 'That ... which we have heard, which we have seen with our eyes, which we have beheld and our hands have touched, concerning the Logos of life; for the life was manifested, and we have seen it and we bear witness and declare to you the life everlasting, which was with the Father and has appeared to us.' (I John 1:1-2)

This vision of the glory of God, and the most sweet visitations of Christ, justify all the monk's apostolic struggles and make the monastic life the 'true and blessed life' which he would exchange for nothing other – however lowly he may be, and however short the time he, by God's grace, may have been given to know it.

The monk radiates mystically this grace even to his brothers in the world, so that all may see, may repent, may be consoled, may rejoice in the Lord and glorify the merciful God 'who gives such authority to men'. (Matthew 9:8)

IV

THEOTOKOS: GUIDE TO TRUE FREEDOM

(Christmas Address, 1986)

This year in particular, let us direct our attention to one of the most beautiful idiomela of the Vespers for Christmas:

> What shall we offer Thee, O Christ,
> Who for our sakes hast appeared on earth as man?
> Every creature made by Thee offers Thee thanks.
> The angels offer Thee a hymn; the heavens a star;
> The Magi, goats; the shepherds, their wonder;
> The earth, its cave: the Wilderness, the manger:
> And we offer Thee a Virgin Mother,
> O Pre-Eternal God,
> have mercy on us.

All God's creation feels the need to thank Christ for His Incarnation, and to offer Him the gift of its gratitude. The angels offer their hymns; they awaited the incarnation of Christ because they loved mankind, and were saddened to see men far from God. With the Incarnation and Resurrection of Christ, the good angels will be stabilised in their goodness, that is, holiness and sinlessness and, even more – beatitude and glory will become their permanent condition.

Non-rational creation suffered and groaned with mankind and awaited with yearning (cf. Romans 8:19) the liberation of man and of creation itself from the decay it inherited with man, after his fall and separation from the heavenly Father and creator, the source of life.

Rational man suffered even more, awaiting his liberation. For this reason, mankind offers the highest gift to Christ Who becomes man – His Virgin Mother.

In fact, we men had nothing more honourable to offer God. The Panagia (*Pan Aghia*: 'All Holy Mother of God') had already offered herself entirely to God and as a most pure vessel was ready to receive in her womb her Son and her God. And so, at her Annunciation, when Archangel Gabriel told her that she would become the Mother of Christ, she could answer with confidence in God: 'Behold the handmaid of the Lord. Be it unto me according to thy word.' (Luke 1.38)

Moreover, we could not have offered the Virgin Mary to God if she had not offered herself to God. This free offering of the Virgin Mary made the incarnation of God possible, for God would not violate our freedom by becoming incarnate without our own consent. The Virgin Mary was able to stand before God as our representative, and to say 'Yes' to God. Her deed is a deed of unique responsibility, love, and freedom. She gave God what He Himself did not have – human nature – in order that God might give man what he did not have – theosis. Thus the Incarnation of Christ is not only God's free act of offering to man, it is also a free offering from man to God through the Virgin Mary.

This mutual freedom is the prerequisite for love. God Himself offers freely without any necessity, and the Virgin Mary accepts the gift freely, without compulsion. The Virgin Mary could not co-operate with God if she had established her own egotistic satisfaction as the content of her freedom – rather than her offering to God and man. Moreover, the Virgin Mary is always rightly blessed by all generations of Christians, and especially during these holy days, as the 'cause of the deification of all'. At the same time, she points out the way of true freedom.

Contemporary man is deluded by the devil and believes – as did Adam and Eve earlier – that his freedom is to be found in his autonomy and in his revolt against God. With this egotistic attitude man loses the possibility of true communion, not only with his God and Father, but also with his fellow men, and he lives as an orphan in an intolerable loneliness, which he experiences as an existential emptiness. A young man who uses drugs assured me that he would stop using them if he could stop trying to fill his emptiness with them.

The Virgin Mary, Panagia, and her Incarnate Son call us to the freedom of love. This freedom proceeds from the Cross. This is not the easy way of the satisfaction of our passions. It is the hard way of sacrifice, of offering, of victory over egotism.

In the name of this freedom, which we have received from the Gospel of Christ, and from the tradition of our Greek Orthodox people, we cannot accept institutions such as those allowing abortion, which evade the freedom of love and which introduce the 'freedom' of egoism as a way of life. Having chosen the freedom of love as a way of life in the world, as inaugurated in this world by the Virgin Mary and her Only-Begotten Son, we Orthodox Christians have before us a great struggle: for we must strive to acquire this freedom. This is the struggle of the Orthodox Christian. This struggle is a Cross – but it is also a joyful struggle because it carries us to the Resurrection.

In this struggle, which you also undergo, we pray that our Saviour Jesus Christ, Who was born in a cave, will grant you His Grace and blessing, through the intercessions of His most blessed Mother and our Mother, the Lady Theotokos.

GLOSSARY

Essence (οὐσία-ousia)
God's essence and His energies are pre-eternal and uncreated. God's essence, that is His essential nature, is inaccessible and unknowable to us, and therefore will always remain a mystery.

The distinction between God's essence and His energies guarantees God's unknowability, whilst simultaneously giving us the possibility to achieve intimate and personal communion with Him through His energies, which are accessible to us.

Heart (καρδία-kardia)
The heart is a biblical word little understood these days, yet it has a truly profound dimension. The heart is where union with God may be consummated; as such it has a spiritual dimension. More than an emotional centre, or a physical organ, the heart is a receptacle for all good and evil. The heart is our psychosomatic centre, the deepest and most profound part of our being; it is our inner man, out of which the energies of the psyche issue forth. There is a close connection between the nous, the psyche, the heart, and the inner man.

Hesychia (ἡσυχία-hesychia)
Silence, stillness. Stilling of the thoughts, but not emptiness, whereby the nous may descend into the heart through the Jesus prayer. Hesychia deifies, according to St. Gregory the

Theologian, because it helps us to truly know ourselves and also our God.

Kingdom of God (Βασιλεία τοῦ Θεοῦ–Basileia tou Theou)
The Kingdom of God means, the 'Rule of God', and also the 'Ruling power of God'. Although it is all-pervading and ever-present, it is spiritual and beyond all sensible and intelligible categories. The Kingdom of God also refers to our participation in the divine life of the Holy Trinity, making the chosen person through Grace what God is by nature. The Kingdom of God and the Kingdom of Heaven are synonymous.

St. Symeon the New Theologian describes it in the following way: 'For those who become children of light and sons of the day to come, for those who always walk in the light, the Day of the Lord will never come, for they are already with God and in God.'

Logos (Λόγος–Logos)
The Greek word logos already had a long history before it was used by St. John. Its three principle meanings are: think, reckon, and speak. Like all things rational, logos at its most profound level conveys: the meaning, the ordering, and reasonable content. In time, this also came to be identified with Universal Reason, and Creative Reason.

St. John completes the philosophical truths of the Ancient Greeks by connecting them to the Jewish tradition of his day. St. John's Gospel tells us: 'In the beginning was the Logos, and the Logos was with God, and the Logos was God. He was in the beginning with God. All things were made through Him, and without Him was not anything made that was made. In Him exists life, and the life was the light of men. And the Logos became flesh and dwelt among us.' (John 1:1) Here, St. John clearly states that Jesus Christ is both the Logos and YHWH. The Logos, the second Person of the Holy Trinity, is also known as the Wisdom, Intellect and Providence of God. It is in the Logos that creation finds its reason, cause, and purpose.

Man (ἄνθρωπος–anthropos)

Along with the Holy Bible, theology frequently uses the word man in a generic sense for both man and woman. Man is the only creature to be made in the image and likeness of God (Genesis 1:26), and as such was God's crowning achievement. God's vision of humanity far exceeds our limited understanding and this can partly be seen in Christ's saying: 'For in the resurrection they neither marry nor are given in marriage, but are like angels of God in heaven.' (Matthew 22:30)

Mystery (μυστήριον–mysterion)

The Greek word 'mystery' originally meant initiation, secret, or revelation of a secret. Christianity inherited this meaning, and by extension it came to mean 'revelation from God'.

The Mysteries are both a symbol and a mystery. As long as the mystery remains 'veiled' the rituals remain on the symbolic and iconographic level; but when one is receptive and Grace acts, then the Mysteries reveal that which is behind the 'veil'. Mystery carries the duel connotation of something both hidden and revealed, both a riddle and a revelation together.

The two main mysteries that were established by Christ are Baptism and the Holy Eucharist. There are now seven main liturgical mysteries, but their number is potentially limitless, because in the Church all things work in a mysterious way to reveal the Kingdom of God.

Nepsis (νῆψις–nepsis; adjective: neptic)

Nepsis is vigilance of the nous and watchfulness at the gates of the heart, so that every thought that moves in it can be controlled.

Nous (νοῦς–nous)

The nous is our highest faculty. It has been called: the eye of the psyche, the eye of the heart, and also the energy of the psyche. When cleansed, the nous resides and operates from within the heart; it can perceive God and the spiritual principles that underlie creation; it is cognitive, visionary, and intuitive. The Metropolitan Hierotheos of Nafpaktos said: 'The nous is in the image of God. And inasmuch as God is light, the nous too has light mirrored in it by the Grace of God.'

After man's fall and the fragmentation of the psyche, the nous will invariably identify itself with the mind, the imagination, the senses, or even the body, so losing sight of its pure unalloyed state.

Psyche (ψυχή–psyche)

The most important and least understood of all Biblical words is the word psyche. The Orthodox understanding of psyche remains unified and unchanged. In order to encapsulate the full meaning of the word psyche as understood by traditional Christianity, we will have to combine the meanings of five English words: 'soul', 'life', 'breath', 'psyche' and 'mind'.

In the West, 'soul' has become a debased and ambiguous term; the psyche, its original biblical counterpart, has now constellated into two distinct conceptual fields. The words 'soul', 'life', and 'breath' form one field. The words 'psyche' (as in modern psychology), and 'mind' (as in the mind-body dichotomy) comprise the other field. As such, there is little or no connection between psychic health and the eternal animating principle known as soul. This dislocation is indicative of a deep spiritual malady in Western man.

The psyche is not only that individual immortal part of us, our immaterial nature, that which animates the body and gives it life. It also conveys the meaning breath, whilst also comprising of our cognitive, conative, and affective aspects, including both the conscious and the unconscious.

Repentance (μετάνοια–metanoia)

Repentance means: a change of heart, a change of mind – its literal meaning is a change of nous (i.e. meta-nous). Repentance is more than regret or contrition – it requires a fundamental change of life.

Christ tells us that the path for approaching the Kingdom of God is repentance. A more accurate translation of Matthew 4:17 is '*keep repenting*, for the Kingdom is at hand'; in other words, not once, but continually. We must continually re-direct ourselves, until we achieve life's objective – union with God. As such, repentance is a mystery.

Repentance is not legalistic; i.e. if a penance is given during confession by the spiritual confessor, this will be purely for therapeutic reasons, whose aim is to clear the nous and the heart from sin.

Sin (ἁμαρτία–hamartia)

In Christianity, hamartia means 'estrangement from God,' or more accurately 'failure to achieve one's destiny'. Correspondingly, the verb harmartanein means 'to fall short of one's destiny' – the original meaning was to miss the mark. These words were later translated as 'sin' and 'to sin'.

The primary objective of human life is to unite with God: so any action or even thought that estranges us from God is a sin. As St. Paul tells us: 'The sting of death is sin.'

(I Corinthians 16:56) Sin has no legalistic dimension: it is simply the estrangement from Life.

Theology, Theologian (θεολόγος–theologos)

Theology deals with God, our participation in Him, and the underlying divine reality inherent in creation. It is far more than intellectual and scholarly discourse about God, and is not acquired through academic study.

A real theologian is someone who has reached intimate communion with God, and has perception of the spiritual world. To quote Evagrius: 'If you are a theologian, you will pray truly; and if you truly pray, you are a theologian.' St. Maximus the Confessor and St. Gregory Palamas say: 'Our devotion lies not in words but in realities.'

Theosis (θέωσις–Theosis)

Theosis literally means to become gods by Grace. The Biblical words that are synonymous and descriptive of Theosis are: adoption, redemption, inheritance, glorification, holiness and perfection.

Theosis is the acquisition of the Holy Spirit, whereby through Grace one becomes a participant in the Kingdom of God. Theosis is an act of the uncreated and infinite love of God. It begins here in time and space, but it is not static or complete, and is an open-ended progression uninterrupted through all eternity.

Theotokos (Θεοτόκος–Theotokos)

The title Theotokos given to the Virgin Mary means Mother of God; its literal translation is God-birthgiver. This title was affirmed by the third Œcumenical Synod (341 AD) to declare that Christ was truly and fully God even before His incarnation.

The crosses featured as page ornaments on p iii & p vi and the star
on this page are by Andrew Gould, at www.newworldbyzantine.com
and provided by the Orthodox Arts Journal. Many thanks!
All other page ornaments are by Pleroma and were created from
illustrations found in the book *Treasures of Mt Athos*.

www.ingramcontent.com/pod-product-compliance
Lightning Source LLC
Chambersburg PA
CBHW020625300426
44113CB00007B/780